HOW IT WAS
ELIZABETHAN LIFE

Stewart Ross

BT Batsford Ltd , London

CONTENTS

Typeset by Deltatype Limited, Ellesmere Port
and printed in Hong Kong
for the publishers
B. T. Batsford Ltd
4 Fitzhardinge Street
London W1H 0AH

ISBN 0 7134 6356 2

The frontispiece shows A Portrait of a Young Man, *by Isaac Oliver (1556 – 1617). During the Elizabethan age, English miniature painting – paintings only a few centimetres square – became famous throughout Europe. This painting shows an idealized view of both the young man himself, and the architecture and gardens behind him.*

Cover illustration:

Queen Elizabeth being carried in a grand procession in 1600. The importance of the Queen is emphasized by her glorious jewelled clothes. She was personally responsible for the government of her realm.

INTRODUCTION

Elizabeth I was Queen of England and Wales four hundred years ago. She was on the throne for 45 years (1558–1603) and was such an impressive person that we refer to her reign as the 'Elizabethan Age'. It was a period of great excitement. Several times the country was threatened with invasion by foreign armies, but at home there was peace and new prosperity for the wealthier citizens. The population was rising and thousands of new houses were built. Painting, music, architecture and literature all flourished. William Shakespeare, the greatest Elizabethan of all, wrote most of his magnificent plays at this time.

Yet compared with our century life in Elizabethan times was cruel and hard. Most people had scarcely enough food to eat. A wet summer usually meant a bad harvest and starvation for thousands. The poor lived in huts, dressed in rough clothes, and rarely travelled far from the place where they had been born. A man or woman was considered old by the age of forty. Many children died of disease or malnutrition before they became teenagers and little was known of scientific medicine. Can you imagine what life would be like without all the inventions which we take for granted? Most of Elizabethan England's four million inhabitants (ten times less than today) dwelt in tiny hamlets or villages without cars, televisions, electric lights or refrigerators. Lavatories, running water and proper drains were almost unknown.

Although by our standards life in the second half of the sixteenth century was rough, the people who lived then did not know any better. They got on with their daily lives with the same happiness and misery as we do. The vigorous and creative Elizabethans were also very proud of their country. One of Shakespeare's characters speaks affectionately of 'This land of such dear souls, this dear, dear land.' This book will tell you what it was like to live in the land which he loved so much.

Introductory Quiz

Do you know?
What did Queen Elizabeth I look like?

Which country tried to invade England in 1588?

How most people were employed in Elizabethan times?

Did Queen Elizabeth burn people at the stake?

Why some Elizabethans poured fox fat on their heads?

(You will find the answers to these questions and many more in the following pages.)

COUNTRY LIFE

The Elizabethans were countryfolk. About 80 percent of them lived in small rural communities, each with a few hundred inhabitants. Even those who lived in the towns were never more than a few minutes walk from open countryside and most had gardens in which they kept livestock and grew vegetables. They followed the changing seasons; almost everyone knew the names of the trees, birds, herbs and flowers which they came across every day.

Because villages were small and travel was expensive and dangerous, there was a strong sense of belonging to the local community. The words 'county' and 'country' meant much the same thing. Villagers knew about each others' lives and there was a good deal of gossip and squabbling. But locals soon rallied round if they felt threatened by outsiders. The pattern of life changed little and there was not much sense of haste or urgency in the way people went about their daily tasks. They were reminded of the passage of time only by the chimes of the village clock or the position of the sun in the sky.

The two most impressive buildings in the village were the church and the manor house. The Elizabethans were great builders and in the sixteenth century many gentlemen constructed fine new mansions of brick or stone. Since they owned much land and were far wealthier than other villagers, the lords of the manor were feared and respected. They were responsible for settling petty disputes, such as when a farmer had his crops trampled by a neighbour's stray cow. They also had to enforce dozens of laws. These covered a broad range of matters, from ensuring that everyone wore a woollen cap on Sundays (to help the wool industry), to seeing that the village held enough bows and arrows for use in an emergency.

Other important villagers were the blacksmith, the miller and the clergyman. There was no village shop, for families made or grew for themselves most of the things they needed. The local weekly market was central to their lives. Here they sold surplus produce and bought little luxuries or things they could not easily make at home, such as fancy clothing or household items. For the poorer people the social centre of the village was the alehouse or inn where they gathered to swap stories, hear the latest news and rumours, and drink pints of home-brewed beer.

In England's more fertile districts the land around the village was divided into huge open fields in which individual farmers held strips of land. In other parts of the country farms were broken up into the familiar modern patchwork of smaller fields, divided by walls or hedges. Around the fields there were broad common lands for grazing sheep, pigs and cattle. Sometimes these commons were fenced in by the wealthier farmers for their own use. This process, known as enclosure, produced much bitterness among those deprived of their rights.

A sixteenth-century Flemish book illustration showing autumn work on the farm. Can you identify four different activities taking place?

COUNTRY LIFE

There were several types of farmer in Elizabethan times. The *gentry* owned a good deal of land but did not work it themselves. They either leased it to others or employed *bailiffs* to look after their farms and hire *landless labourers* to do the work. These men were paid with food and low wages – about sixpence per day. *Yeomen* owned small farms and, helped by their families, did most of their own work. *Tenants* rented their land for an annual payment in money or goods.

The Harvest

This picture shows a bailiff overseeing labourers at work on the harvest.

Both men and women are at work in the field. Can you identify the different tasks which they are doing? The Elizabethans were very conscious of their class: how can you tell the bailiff from the labourers?

THINGS TO DO

1   The marks left by strip farming can still be seen in some fields. They look like long humps, about 20 metres wide and 200 metres long. See if you can identify them when next you travel through the countryside. They can best be seen when the sun is low.

2   If you can persuade the rest of your family to agree, try spending an hour or so at home in the winter without using either gas or electricity! That will give you some idea what life was like in an ordinary Elizabethan household.

3   Ask at your local library whether there are any Elizabethan manor houses still standing in your district. Find out when they were built.

Why was this time of year a good one for the labourers?

Which months did they not look forward to?

CHECK YOUR UNDERSTANDING

Can you remember the meaning of the following words?

Enclosure

Manor

The common land

Bailiff

Yeoman

Husbandry

Enclosures

The pictures you have seen of country life show most farm work being done by hand. There were very few machines and, as the poorer farmers could not afford to own horses, they either shared them or used oxen instead. On the other hand, cattle or sheep rearing needed only one or two people to tend the animals in the field or cope with the milking. Why do you think some wealthy farmers changed from growing crops to rearing cattle or sheep? Here is a complaint written in 1600 by William Vaughan: what does he say is the result of enclosure?

There is no life more pleasant than a yeoman's life, but nowadays yeomanry is decayed . . . and husbandry [farming] quite fallen. The reason is because landlords . . . do enclose for pasture many thousand acres of ground within one hedge, the husbandmen are thrust out . . .

Q

We now know that the problem was not as serious as William Vaughan made out. Complaints such as his were usually loudest after several years of poor harvests. Why was this?

A fair day's work

Here is a law passed early in the sixteenth century setting out the length of a labourer's day. Can you work out how many hours a day he had to work?

Every . . . labourer shall be at work between the middle of the month of March and the middle of the month of September, before 5 of the clock in the morning. And that he have but half an hour for his breakfast and an hour and a half for his dinner . . . And that he depart not from his work till between 7 and 8 of the clock in the evening.

The rest of the law shows us how, in the days before gas or electric light, everyone was dependent upon daylight:

And for the rest of the year they shall be at their work in the springing of the day [daybreak] and depart not till night of the same day.

(Quoted in *The Tudor Age*, by A.F. Scott)

CAN YOU REMEMBER ?

In what sort of communities did most Elizabethans live: cities, villages or towns?

Had wristwatches been invented in the sixteenth century?

Who was responsible for settling local disputes?

Where did villagers buy goods they could not make themselves?

What was 'strip farming'?

TOWN LIFE

At the time of Queen Elizabeth I about one fifth of the population of England and Wales lived in towns. (Scotland remained an independent country until 1707, over one hundred years after the queen's death.) Apart from London, all towns were very small by our standards – the biggest three were Norwich (about 15,000 inhabitants by 1600), Bristol (12,000) and York (11,500). An important county town like Canterbury boasted only 5000 citizens, while a market town such as Burford (population 800) was little more than a village. Nevertheless, the towns played a major part in Elizabethan life. They were where the markets were held and where the law courts sat. Shops, schools and garrisons of troops were found in the towns, too.

London was quite different from the rest of the country. With a population of over 200,000 it was one of the leading cities in Europe, and it was growing all the time. King James I, who succeeded Elizabeth to the throne in 1603, complained that 'soon London will be all England'. There are four reasons why London had grown to such a size and why it was so important. Firstly, it was well situated for trade with the continent. Secondly, all the major law courts were there. Each year hundreds of lawyers came to the Inns of Court to learn their profession. A third reason for London's importance is that Parliament usually met there, or, to be more accurate, in the suburb known as Westminster. This made the city a focus of attention for the whole nation. Finally, the royal court, which employed hundreds of servants and cost thousands of pounds annually, spent most of its time in the capital.

The queen had two London palaces, Whitehall and St James's. Elizabeth's court was at the centre of government, for in those days the monarch had to govern the country as well as perform all sorts of ceremonial duties. Ambitious and powerful lords and ladies flocked to court, bringing with them their servants. Housing, feeding and providing all the other needs of these people added greatly to London's prosperity. The city's innkeepers, businessmen and shopkeepers all felt the pinch when the court moved off to another part of the country, as it did from time to time.

Several wealthy families had houses in London as well as in the country. The city originally stood within stout walls to the north of London Bridge. It contained the Tower of London and the old St Paul's Cathedral. (The present cathedral was built in the seventeenth century to replace the medieval one which was destroyed in the Great Fire of 1666.) But by Elizabethan times the city had spread beyond the walls, largely to the west towards the royal palaces and the cathedral called Westminster – 'minster' is another word for a church. The fine brick and stone mansions of the nobility and gentry were built in the 'West End'. The servants and poorer people crammed into wooden houses built in higgledy-piggledy fashion all over the great sprawling city.

The old St Paul's Cathedral which was burned down in the great fire of 1666. The building dominated Elizabethan London.

Country people were often attracted to the towns. Life there seemed more exciting, and there was greater opportunity to make money. But the towns were also very dangerous. Fire was a real problem as most houses were built of wood, with thatched roofs. Stratford was devastated by fire in successive years (1594 and 1595). In 1574 Bristol banned the thatching of roofs, while Exeter ordered supplies of buckets, ladders and fire hooks (for pulling down thatched roofs in the path of a fire) to be always at the ready. Suggest reasons why there are so few Elizabethan town houses left standing today.

An ancient timber-framed building being restored. You can imagine why fire was such a hazard in buildings like this.

Muddy Waters

Disease was another problem of town life. Can you imagine the sort of health risks involved in London's water supply, described here by a writer in 1599?

> Spring or drinking water is enclosed in great . . . stone cisterns [tanks] in different parts of the town, [and] is let off through cocks [taps] into special wooden iron-bound vessels with broad bottoms and narrow tops, which poor labourers carry to and fro to the houses on their shoulders . . .

Getting rid of sewage was even more difficult. There were no flushing toilets, just stinking buckets or barrels in the basements of the houses which had to be emptied from time to time. The Fleet ditch, which ran through London, was a popular place for dumping all kinds of rubbish. In 1589 the city government tried to clean it out and make it run with fresh drinking water. What problem did they meet?

> . . . it was undertaken, that by drawing divers [several] springs about Hampstead Heath into one head and course [one channel], . . . the city should be served of fresh water in all places . . . but much money being . . . spent, the effect failed, so that the brook [stream], by means of continual encroachments upon the banks getting over the water*, and casting of soilage into the stream, is now become worse cloyed and choken [blocked] than ever it was before.

continual encroachments getting over the water = with banks always falling in; *cloyed and choken* = *blocked.*

(John Stow, *The Survey of London*, 1599)

Prigmen and Kinching Morts

A third danger in the towns was the number of criminals who gathered there, especially in the larger ones. Those who were out of work, or who had fallen on hard times, often turned to crime. Many had little choice, for they were faced with starvation. The Elizabethans did not have very efficient means of helping the needy. There were vivid names for the different sorts of villains: horse-thieves were known as 'priggers of prancers', those who stole clothes hung out to dry were 'prigmen', criminal girls were 'kinching morts' and women who pretended to have lost all their possessions in a fire were 'demanders for glimmer'. This picture shows the sort of harsh punishment given to criminals who were caught.

CHECK YOUR UNDERSTANDING

Can you remember the meaning of the following words?

The inns of court

Minster

Fire hooks

Brook

Prigmen

CAN YOU REMEMBER ?

What was the population of London in Elizabeth's reign?

Which royal palaces were in London?

Where were markets held?

Why did Bristol ban thatched roofs in 1574?

What happened to the Fleet ditch by the end of Elizabeth's reign?

THINGS TO DO

1   From your local library try to find out the size of your town, or one near you, in Elizabethan times.

2   Look at the map on page 45. Can you think of a modern city which was not important enough in the sixteenth century to be included on the map? Why did it later expand?

3   Is there a market held near where you live? How long has it been held in the same place? Your teacher, library or local tourist office may be able to help.

On the northern frontier with Scotland, those who could afford to still lived in castles or fortified houses. In the rest of the country it was different: houses were built for comfort and show. The grandest house of the Elizabethan age was Burghley House, built by Elizabeth's leading minister, William Cecil. You can see a picture of it on the opposite page. Although some buildings were constructed of stone or warm red brick, most were put up on a wooden frame. Many of the attractive houses with black beams and white plaster which you can see today were built by Elizabethans. The poorer people had only tiny cottages (called 'cotes'), without chimneys or glass in the windows. Open fires were used for cooking and keeping a house warm. Coal was becoming a popular fuel, particularly in the towns.

The Elizabethans knew little about healthy eating. The better-off classes consumed huge quantities of meat but not enough fruit or vegetables. This made them liable to suffer from scurvy, a disease which probably killed Elizabeth's father, Henry VIII. Poorer people ate whatever they could get hold of. Rabbits and pigeons were popular catches but the staple (main) food of the masses was bread. White bread made from wheat was expensive, so the poor bought brown bread baked from barley or rye flour.

Since it was not easy to keep animals over the long dark months of winter, most had to be slaughtered in the autumn and their meat preserved by salting or smoking. As there was no canning or refrigeration, winter food was limited in choice and low on important vitamins. Meals were served on wooden platters, and eaten with the hands and a knife. Forks and glasses were rare. Beer was the most popular drink, although the wealthier classes drank wine imported from France.

The Elizabethans were very conscious of their position in society. Each person was expected to wear clothes suitable to his or her class, and those who dressed 'above themselves' could be punished! In the picture of the banquet on page 13 you can see the clothes which better-off people dressed in. Everyone wore a hat of some sort. For much of the period it was fashionable for men and women to wear a huge puffed-up collar, known as a ruff. Women wore long dresses with exaggerated waists,

Burghley House in Lincolnshire, built by Lord Burghley, Elizabeth's Lord Treasurer. An army of servants was needed to run the house, which was more like a village than a home.

below which they were not expected to show more than their ankles.

The pattern of daily life in a household was set by the hours of daylight. Men went out to work soon after sunrise and did not return until dark. As candles were not cheap the poor went to bed early in the winter, or sat chatting by the fire. Housework was done by hand. A family employed servants if it could afford to. They usually slept in the attic or in an outhouse. Most women, however, had to do their own washing and cleaning, as well as spinning, weaving, sewing or taking in extra washing to earn some money. The idea of going away for a holiday was unknown, but there were about thirty 'holy-days' when the Elizabethans devoted themselves to fun and games (see page 30).

An Elizabethan banquet. The guests are being entertained by actors and musicians performing a short drama known as a masque.

A Merchant's Wife

For the nobility, gentry, merchantmen and businessmen the sixteenth century was a time of growing prosperity. This can be seen in their fine houses and in many other ways, as the extracts in this spread show.

Why is this middle-class lady considered a snob?

Mistress Minx, a merchant's wife, that [who] will eat no cherries . . . but [except] when they are at twenty shillings* a pound [and] . . . will not go into the fields, to cower [squat] on the green grass, but she must have a coach for her convoy [conveyance].

*a shilling, made up of twelve old pennies, was 1/20 of £1.00.

Drinking glasses, imported from abroad, were very expensive but highly fashionable: 'Glasses, glasses, is the only drinking,' said Sir John Falstaff in Shakespeare's *Henry IV*, part ii.

Food, Glorious Food

No one ate better than the well-to-do English:

In number of dishes and change of meat the nobility of England . . . do . . . exceed, sith* there is no day in manner that passeth over their heads wherein they have not only beef, mutton, veal, lamb, kid, pork, cony*, capon, pig . . . also some portion of the red or fallow deer, beside a great variety of fish and wild-fowl.

sith = so that; cony = rabbit.

THINGS TO DO

1 Find out all you can about the disease scurvy. What causes it and how can it be cured?

2 Try and find as many pictures as you can of Elizabethan houses. Study them carefully and draw all the different shapes of chimney you can see.

3 What were the ancient 'holy-days', when people did not work? How many of them remain as our bank holidays?

Elizabethan Fashions

As always, time and money were spent on fashions.

[Women] . . . are not simply content with their own hair, but buy other hair, either of horses, mares, or any other strange beast, dying it of what colour they list [want] themselves. And if there be any poor woman . . . that hath fair hair, these nice* dames will not rest till they have bought it.

*'nice' is used here in a sarcastic way.

Another writer complained:

The fantastical folly [stupidity] of our nation (even from the courtier to the carter), is such that no form of apparel [dress] liketh us longer than the first garment is in the wearing [we like an article of clothing only for the first time we put it on].

(All quotes on this page come from *The Tudor Age*)

Rich Man, Poor Man

The increasing wealth of some folk, with their feasting and fine clothes, made the condition of the poor seem worse. In hard times people in authority were afraid of rebellion. Much teaching, especially in church, urged people to accept their position in life because it was given by God. It did not much matter what happened on earth, whether one was rich or poor, because the really important thing was to lead a good life and get to heaven when one died.

The rich were also urged to give charity ('alms') to the poor. Can you see how they are helping the poor in this picture?

CAN YOU REMEMBER ?

Which fuel were the Elizabethans beginning to use in large quantities?

From which cereal crops did the poor make their bread?

What was the most popular drink in Elizabethan times?

What were the most fashionable drinking vessels?

Why did the wealthy give generously to the poor and teach that God gave everyone their place in society?

CHECK YOUR UNDERSTANDING

Can you remember the meaning of the following words?

Cote	Shilling
Scurvey	Cony
Staple food	Alms
Ruff	

WOMEN AND CHILDREN

Although in the later sixteenth century England was ruled by a queen, women were seen as inferior to men. They were thought weaker, less intelligent and prone to evil. One important reason for this was the teaching of the church, which believed every word in the Bible to be true. Women were criticized in the story of Genesis. This told that evil entered the world because Eve had been tempted by a snake in the garden of Eden, then persuaded Adam to join her in sin. All important jobs were reserved for men. Women were not even allowed on stage: female parts in plays were acted by boys.

Before they were married most girls left home to work as servants in large households, inns or similar places. The work was hard and the hours were long. They were given little free time and had to behave themselves properly. On average women married in their early twenties and men about five years later. They were not expected to marry until they could support themselves. This often meant that a man had to wait until his father died or retired. Parents usually had to approve or even arrange their children's marriages. Few couples married purely for love.

Most women had about six children but at least a quarter of them died before reaching the age of ten. Therefore, households were not much larger than they are today, especially as older children left home to work. Childbirth was very dangerous, without pain-relieving drugs (anaesthetics) or proper medical assistance. Many women died while giving birth, or shortly afterwards. As well as the baptism ceremony for a baby, there was a special church service for women who had just produced a child; it was known as the 'churching of women'.

It is not easy for us to find out what the Elizabethans thought of children. As in our century, some were dearly loved, while in other families they were maltreated and neglected. Corporal punishment was used much more than today. Young babies were wrapped tightly in what were known as swaddling clothes, which made them look like tiny ancient Egyptian mummies. Older children wore miniature versions of adult clothes. Towards the end of the century, however, they began to have special loose-fitting clothes of their own.

The only time that many families came together was for prayers in the morning and evening. When their father was around children had to behave politely, not making a noise or speaking unless spoken to. Wives, too, were expected to obey their husbands in all matters. Divorce was almost unknown. These practices seem unfair to us but they were accepted as normal by Elizabethans. As the monarch ruled the kingdom, so the husband ruled the family.

Part of a painting entitled 'Children's Games', produced in 1560 by Pieter Bruegel. How many of the games can you recognize?

WOMEN AND CHILDREN

One of the most horrifying aspects of Elizabethan life was the belief in witchcraft. It led to many innocent women being persecuted or even killed.

Witches

What is a witch?

> . . . one that worketh by the Devil . . . either hurting or healing, revealing things secret or foretelling things to come, which the Devil hath devised to entangle and snare men's sails withal* unto damnation . . .
>
> *to entangle and snare men's sails withal = by this means trap men's souls.
>
> A witch or hag is she which, being deluded [deceived] by a league made with the devil . . . thinketh she can design [arrange] what manner of evil things soever . . . as to shake the air with lightnings and thunder, to cause hail and tempests, to remove green corn or trees to another place, to be carried . . . into some mountain far distant, in a wonderful short space of time, and sometimes to fly upon a staff . . .

(Quoted in *The Tudor Age*)

Which phrase in the first passage tells us that witches did not only do evil?

How does the second passage differ from the first one?

Women at Work

Elizabethan women carrying hay. Among the poorer sections of society women were expected to work as well as look after the home and the children. They certainly did not enjoy equal rights with men.

Accused of Witchcraft

Witches could be young and beautiful, old and crabby, physically deformed or mentally ill. There were many reasons why suspicious or frightened neighbours might accuse a woman of being in league with the devil. It wasn't always for doing evil that someone might be thought a witch. Once accused, it was difficult for a victim to escape, as this story of Geillis Duncane shows:

> Within the town of Trenent . . . there dwelleth . . . a maid called Geillis Duncane, who used secretly to absent [go out] . . . of her master's house every other night. [She] . . . took in hand to help all such as were troubled or grieved with any kind of sickness or infirmity, and in short space did perform many matters most miraculous . . . Whereupon, her master began to grow very inquisitive, and examined her . . . by what means she was able to perform matters of so great importance; . . . she gave him no answer. Nevertheless, her master . . . did with the help of others torment her with the torture of pilliwinks* upon her fingers, which is a grievous torture; and binding or wrenching her head with a cord or rope, which is a most cruel torment also . . .

> *pilliwinks = instruments to crush the finger bones.

> (Quoted in *The Tudor Age*)

Is it surprising that in the end the poor girl confessed to being a witch?

CHECK YOUR UNDERSTANDING

Can you remember the meaning of the following words?

Anaesthetic

Churching of women

Swaddling clothes

CAN YOU REMEMBER ?

Why did Elizabethans believe that the Bible story of Adam and Eve supported the idea that women were weaker and more wicked than men?

What was the average age at which men and women were married in the sixteenth century?

Why was childbirth so dangerous in Elizabethan times?

For whom were witches supposed to work?

Why did many women accused of witchcraft admit the charges made against them?

THINGS TO DO

1 Find out as much as you can about the ancient belief in witchcraft. Is it mentioned in Shakespeare's plays? When did people stop executing women for being witches?

2 Make a study of women's dress in Elizabethan times. Try to find out the reasons why different clothes were worn. The books mentioned in the 'Further Reading' section at the end of this book will help you. You may be able to find some of them in your school or town library.

EDUCATION

In Elizabethan England the ability to read and write (known as literacy) was not as widespread as today. There were more literate people in the south, particularly in London, than in the north; the nobility, gentry and merchants were better educated than the common people. By and large men received better schooling than women.

By 1600 all men and women of the upper class could read and write, not only in English, but often in Latin and modern foreign languages. Most of them were also taught music, a little mathematics and history. The sons of some nobility were sent away to boarding school, but most were taught at home by private tutors. At about the age of twelve they were then packed off to a great household to learn the skills expected of a young gentleman: riding, hunting, shooting, and hawking (catching birds with trained hawks). They were also taught formal manners and soldiering.

By the end of Elizabeth's reign it was usual for the sons of the wealthy to attend Oxford or Cambridge (the only universities), or the London Inns of Court or chancery. At university they brushed up their Latin and acquired some knowledge of Greek, classical learning, mathematics and philosophy. The training at London's Inns was in the law. However, there were other colleges in the capital which taught more modern subjects, such as geography and navigation.

The country was dotted with schools of one sort or another. Some parishes had their own elementary schools, while many county towns had a grammar school. In the early part of the century all education had been in the hands of the church. This was changing by Elizabeth's time, when not all teachers were clergymen. There was some instruction in practical subjects, such as keeping accounts. Most schools charged fees.

For boys and the handful of girls lucky enough to attend school the day was long and tiring. It started very early in the morning and went on until early evening. Much of the work consisted in learning by heart long passages from the Bible or ancient authors. In the old-fashioned schools the pupils were permitted to speak nothing but Latin. They were beaten with a birch whip if they were caught breaking this rule. Indeed, there was a good deal of brutal punishment in Elizabethan schools, delivered for the slightest error of memory or manners. Most schoolmasters believed firmly in the old saying, 'Spare the rod and spoil the child'.

Schooling was largely for members of the yeoman class and above. In the north of England only one in ten labourers knew how to sign their name, although more could do so in the south. By the end of Elizabeth's reign, more people were able to read and write than had been able to do so when she came to the throne in 1558. This was such an important change that some scholars have claimed that a revolution was taking place in education.

The King's School, Canterbury,
which was refounded by
Elizabeth's father, Henry VIII. The
school still uses some of the old
monastic buildings which had been
taken from the church in the 1530s.
In Elizabethan times the school day
began with prayers at 6 am and
ended with another service at 5 pm
in the evening.

EDUCATION

Of the three core subjects in our national curriculum (English, Mathematics and Science) only Science did not exist in its modern form in Elizabethan times.

Religion, Magic and Science

In trying to understand the world about them the Elizabethans muddled religion and magic with guesswork and observation. Much of the work of so-called scientists involved astrology (the study of the influence of the planets on our lives) and alchemy (the search for a 'philosopher's stone' which would give eternal life and change ordinary metals into gold and silver). The Polish astronomer Copernicus made this original suggestion in 1543, fifteen years before Elizabeth came to the throne, in his book *On The Revolution of Celestial Bodies*.

I believe we must investigate whether the earth . . . can be thought of as a planet . . . if we admit that the sun is fixed, and recognize that it is the earth rather than the sun which makes an annual revolution, our observations of the movements of stars and planets make just as much sense . . . and it becomes clear that the sun is the centre of the universe . . .

Q

Why do you think that it was more than eighty years before Copernicus's idea was widely accepted?

Which groups of people do you imagine opposed him?

Cures and Remedies

Most Elizabethan medicine was very crude. There were no antiseptics or painkillers. A patient who had to have a leg or arm amputated was usually made drunk, then held down while the surgeon (often the local barber) cut the limb off with a saw. If the patient survived the shock, the stump was painted with hot pitch. Fox grease was seen as a remedy for baldness, and pigeon dung was put on cuts. All kinds of herbal remedies were used, some better than others. Mentally ill people were treated like children. They were given toys to play with and whipped when they misbehaved.

Here is a little rhyme by an Elizabethan doctor.

What do you think it is saying about doctors and their attitude to the plague? Which class of people were in most danger from disease?

And in the time of pestilent plague*
When doctors all did fly* . . .
The Lord appointed me to stay
To cure the sick and sore,
But not the rich and mighty ones
But the distressed poor.

(Quoted in *The Tudor Age*)

*pestilent plague = an outbreak of highly infectious disease; *fly* = run away.

Medical Studies

The picture below is of John Bannister lecturing on anatomy (how the body is made up of different organs) in London in 1581.

Do you think that anatomists were trying to take a careful and logical approach to their subject? A number of things about the picture strike us as strange; study it carefully and consider the following points: the sex of the students; what the people are wearing (clothes and jewelry); the precautions taken against infection from the corpse.

CAN YOU REMEMBER ?

Which classes of people were literate?

Where in London did students learn the law?

Which organization controlled education in the early part of the sixteenth century?

What proportion of workers in the north of England could sign their names?

What was Copernicus's great discovery?

Who often acted as the local surgeon? How did he carry out an amputation?

CHECK YOUR UNDERSTANDING

Can you remember the meaning of the following words?

Literacy

Hawking

Astrology

Alchemy

Anatomy

Plague

THINGS TO DO

1 Find a shop near you that sells herbal remedies and ask those serving if they know for how long their medicines have been used. Make a list of medicines which were used in Elizabethan times and say what they are used for.

2 Draw a picture of an Elizabethan schoolroom. List all the differences between it and your school.

THE POOR

Wherever one looked in Elizabethan times one saw poor people. There were beggars in the streets, vagabonds (rough tramps) roaming the highways, homeless women and children on every hand. The problem was most noticeable in the towns, especially London. Some parts of the capital must have appeared like a struggling third world city today, such as Calcutta. The number of Elizabethan poor was not fixed: when harvest was good and trade was flourishing there was work and food for most people. When times were hard, however, up to a quarter of the population found themselves destitute (without the means to live). They faced starvation.

Throughout the Elizabethan period the parliament and local authorities issued many laws to deal with the problem of the poor. In 1601, right at the end of the queen's reign, one Act (parliamentary law) brought together many previous ideas on the matter. Firstly, each parish was to be responsible for its own paupers. All those who could afford it had to pay a sum of money, known as a rate, towards helping the local poor. A parish overseer saw that money was collected and distributed fairly. Secondly, a distinction was made between the unfortunate poor, who could not help their condition, and those who were too lazy to work. Do you think that this was fair? Would it be easy to decide who was lazy? Fit and strong people without work were to be whipped and sent back to the parish where they came from. Finally, each parish was to provide work for the unemployed. This could be done in a special workhouse and was often very tedious, such as making sacks. Parishes could also set up houses of correction for those who refused to work.

Did these measures do much to help poor people? As far as we can tell they did little to deal with the causes of the problem and they did not assist the unemployed much. Obvious cases of hardship, such as widows left with young children when their husbands died, were probably looked after fairly well in many parishes. People felt sorry for them. But at least half the poor were men and women without education or training, who could not find satisfactory regular work. They attracted little sympathy and the law treated them as criminals.

Why were the Elizabethans so concerned about the poor? Obviously, many better-off families were distressed to see fellow human beings suffering through cold, malnutrition (not having enough good food to eat) and hardship. The church taught Christian kindness, urging believers to be generous to those worse off than themselves. But all those who enjoyed a reasonable standard of living, from the queen to the humblest yeoman, were also afraid of the poor. The huge differences between the wealthy and the paupers made people very angry. The rich were worried that at any moment the lower classes might call for a more just society and rise in bloody rebellion.

A swineherd, one of the lowest paid jobs in Elizabethan England. If a man such as this lost his job he faced almost certain starvation.

THE POOR

In 1600 a labourer's wages could buy him about half as much as they had bought one hundred years previously. Wages had not kept up with the large price rises. During the reign of Queen Elizabeth, therefore, the problem of the poor became more serious.

Who were the Poor?

In 1572 a law divided the poor into groups. Can you say what they were?

> . . . the poor is commonly divided into three sorts, . . . some are poor by impotency [weakness], as the father-less child, the aged, blind and lame . . . ; the second are poor by casualty, as the wounded soldier . . . and the sick person visited [afflicted] with grievous and painful diseases; the third consisteth of thriftless [lazy] poor, as the rioter . . . , the vagabond . . . and . . . the rogue and strumpet [prostitute] . . .

You will notice that the Act does not mention the idea of someone being unemployed.

(From *Statutes of the Realm*, Volume 4, 1572)

Begging

Elizabethans assumed that all those who were fit ought to work, and could do so. However, we know that there were not always enough jobs for everyone, particularly as the population was rising. For example, what happened to a farm labourer if his employer decided to change from growing crops on his land to keeping sheep? When this happened the employee had to try to find work elsewhere. He might go to a nearby town. If he did not soon find a job there he had little alternative but to beg or turn to crime.

In desperation beggars sometimes mutilated themselves or their children to attract sympathy:

> . . . as by making of corrosives and applying the same to the more fleshy parts of their bodies . . . thereby to raise pitiful and odious sores and move the hearts of the goers by . . .

(Quoted in *The Tudor Age*)

CAN YOU REMEMBER ?

Why was the number of poor people in Elizabethan England rising?

What were the three points set out in the 1601 Poor Law?

Why were the Elizabethans so concerned about the poor?

Whom did the Elizabethans blame for unemployment?

What punishments were given to the 'idle poor'?

Branded as Rogues

The punishment was very severe for rogues and others considered to be too idle to work:

> The rogue being apprehended [arrested], committed to prison, and tried . . . if he happen to be convicted for a vagabond . . . he is then immediately adjudged to be grievously whipped and burned through the gristle of the right ear with an hot iron of the compass [size] of an inch about.

Here is a picture of two unfortunate men being 'whipped at the cart tail'. They are tied to the end of the cart and flogged as the vehicle moves about the town or village.

Why do you think the punishment was widely displayed like this? What sort of effect do you think it had on the victims?

> A person convicted a second time of the same offence

> . . . shall then be whipped again, bored likewise through the other ear . . .

(from *Statutes of the Realm*)

Q

What do you think an employer would think of a man with both his ears bored through who came for a job?

A vagrant could be hanged for a third offence.

CHECK YOUR UNDERSTANDING

Can you remember the meaning of the following words?

Vagabond

Destitute

Act

Workhouse

Malnutrition

Apprehend

THINGS TO DO

1   Write a brief story of a day in the life of an imaginary beggar in Elizabethan times.

2   Find out what happens to people who are unemployed today. Compare what you find with what happened four hundred years ago.

3   Elizabethan England suffered from inflation. What is inflation? What effect does it have on a country?

ART AND ENTERTAINMENT

Entertainment in Elizabethan times was vigorous, varied and, at times, dangerous and bloodthirsty. Ordinary people had to manufacture their own amusements because there was no television or radio and cheap books were not available. They played cards or dice, chess or draughts, either at home or in the ale house, where they could also drink and join in the singing. In fine weather they could practise archery, fishing or wrestling. The young might enjoy one of the huge, wild games of football which were played between one village and another. There were few rules: the ball could be picked up and opponents knocked out of the way as play surged over an area covering hundreds of metres.

From time to time travelling entertainers visited a village. They might be 'players' (actors) performing in the open on a hastily drawn up stage. The plays they acted were normally simple tales or versions of well-known stories. Jugglers and acrobats also toured the countryside. In the towns there was bull or bear baiting and cock fighting. Bears were chained to a pole and set upon by fierce dogs; in a cock fight two birds were shod with metal spurs, placed in a ring and allowed to peck and scratch each other to death.

Most executions took place in the open air. Huge crowds assembled to watch unfortunate men and women being beheaded, burned, hanged or tortured to death. The worst punishment was reserved for a traitor. He was hung slowly, then let down while still alive. Next his stomach and intestines were pulled out from a cut in his abdomen. The dead body was

then beheaded and the corpse cut into four pieces, which were displayed on spikes as a warning to others against committing the same crime. The terrible process was known as hanging, drawing and quartering.

Not all entertainment was violent. At fairs there were dances, songs and games of skill. By the end of Elizabeth's reign there were fine theatres in London. The best known is the Globe, where Shakespeare's plays were performed. The theatre brought together men and women of all classes. Normally, however, the gentry and nobility did not mix with the lower classes in their entertainment. Wealthy men enjoyed hunting, duelling and, less frequently, jousting. Women also enjoyed hunting but normally they followed gentler pursuits like embroidery and dancing. Many educated people of both sexes wrote poetry and music – Elizabeth's father was a talented composer and the queen herself performed skilfully on the virginals (an early form of piano).

Most aspects of English culture blossomed during the Elizabethan age. The composers Thomas Tallis and his pupil William Byrd, patronized (employed) by the queen, produced great music. English miniature painting was admired throughout Europe, and, as we have seen (on page 4), fine buildings were erected all over the country. The literature of the Elizabethan age is some of the finest in the English language.

A group of nobles hunting in front of Nonsuch Palace, Elizabeth's favourite residence. Hunting, known as the 'chase', was the most popular sport among men of the upper classes. They hunted deer, foxes and otters.

Theatres

This is one of the few pictures we have of an Elizabethan theatre:

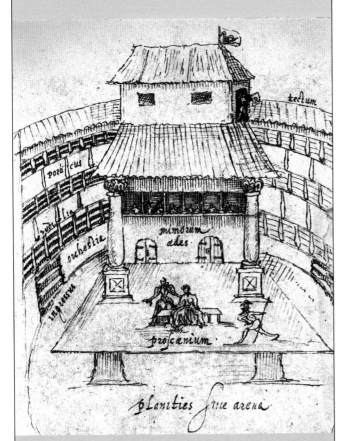

There was very little scenery, so the actors had to rely on their skill and the popularity of the play to hold the audience's attention. Poorer people, known as the 'groundlings', sat on the ground round the edge of the stage. They would boo, hiss and even throw things if they did not like what was being performed. But most of the time they thoroughly enjoyed themselves:

Without [outside] the city are some theatres, where English actors represent almost every day comedies and tragedies to very numerous audiences; these are concluded with variety of dancers, accompanied by excellent music and the excessive applause of those that are present.

[A visitor to London, 1598]

A Cruel Spectacle

A good many Elizabethan entertainments would not be permitted today. They were horribly cruel:

. . . the bears were brought forth into the court, the dogs set to them . . . If the dog would pluck the bear by the throat, the bear would claw him again by the scalp . . . Thus with plucking and tugging, scratching and biting, by plain tooth and nail on one side and the other, such expense of blood and leather was there between them . . . It was a sport very pleasant . . .

(Quoted in *The Tudor Age*)

What was this sport called?

CAN YOU REMEMBER ?

Why was Elizabethan football so dangerous?

What was the favourite outdoor sport of the upper classes?

How were traitors executed?

Name two well-known Elizabethan composers.

For what type of painting is the Elizabethan age most famous?

Foul Play

Elizabethans were no strangers to football violence:

As for concerning football playing, I protest unto you it may rather be called a friendly kind of fight, than a play of recreation; . . . For doth not everyone lie in wait for his adversary [enemy], seeking to overthrow him and to pick [drop] him on his nose, though it be upon hard stones, in ditch or dale . . . ? So . . . sometimes their necks are broken, sometimes their backs, sometimes their legs . . . sometimes their noses gush out with blood, sometimes their eyes start out . . .

CHECK YOUR UNDERSTANDING

Can you remember the meaning of the following words?

Players

Hanging, Drawing and quartering

Groundlings

Virginals

Patronize

Bear-baiting

THINGS TO DO

1 Find out what an Elizabethan theatre looked like and draw a labelled diagram of one.
2 Look up the meaning of the word 'Renaissance'. How did it influence the work of English architects and artists at this time?
3 Listen to some Elizabethan music. What musical instruments were used in the sixteenth century?

A New Discovery

By the very end of Elizabeth's reign, there was a new relaxation to indulge in:

. . . the English are constantly smoking tobacco, and in this manner: they have pipes on purpose made [specially made] of clay, into the farther end of which they put the herb, so dry that it may be rubbed into powder, and putting fire to it, they draw the smoke into their mouths, which they puff out again through their nostrils, like funnels . . .

(Quoted in C. Hole, *England Home Life 1500–1800*)

It was not until this century that doctors began to realize the certain damage which smoking does to people's health.

THE CHURCH AND FAITH

Religion was more important to the Elizabethans than it is to most people today. There was much that the queen and her subjects (those she ruled) did not understand about the world. But their Christian faith helped them to accept its uncertainty and hardships. They believed that life on earth was unimportant compared with life after death. So it didn't matter whether one was rich or poor, happy or unhappy, as long as one had faith in God and lived free from sin. This earned a believer eternal life and a place in heaven.

England was a Roman Catholic country until the time of Elizabeth's father. The Pope was accepted as ruler of the church. But Henry VIII had a bitter argument with the Pope and rejected his leadership of the church. During the reign of Elizabeth's brother, Edward VI (1547–1553), parliament and the government began to change the faith of the English church from Roman Catholicism to Protestantism. However, Elizabeth's sister Mary, who was queen from 1553 to 1558, was a devout Roman Catholic. She made the church Roman Catholic again.

Queen Elizabeth was a Protestant. One of the first things she did when she came to the throne was to get parliament to pass laws making the Church of England Protestant once more. This was done by the Act of Supremacy and the Act of Uniformity. Today's Church of England is basically the same as that which Elizabeth established. The queen was not too concerned with what people believed in their hearts, as long as they all followed the same outward practices. Religion was too important for her to allow every individual to worship as they pleased. The church owned much land, which made it very wealthy. The queen kept in touch with her subjects through its bishops and priests. Sermons were one of the few ways of passing on information from the government to the people. Much education was controlled by the church and it was compulsory to attend its services.

Not everyone agreed with the church which Elizabeth had set up. The Roman Catholics considered the queen a heretic (someone with a false belief). In 1570 the Pope announced that it would not be a sin for a Roman Catholic to assassinate her. Hundreds of Roman Catholic priests were smuggled into England to convert the English back to their old faith. They were not very successful in their mission and many were executed for treason.

There were Protestants, too, who did not agree with the new Church of England. They complained that it still had some Roman Catholic features, such as bishops. The reformers who wanted to purify the

new church were called 'puritans'. Some puritans worked from within the Church of England. One of them, Edmund Grindal, became Archbishop of Canterbury in 1576. The queen suspended him from his duties one year later because he would not do exactly as she wished. Other puritans tried unsuccessfully to set up rival churches.

A picture painted during the reign of Elizabeth's brother Edward VI (1547–1553). It shows the young Protestant king rejecting the Pope.

THE CHURCH AND FAITH

In the sixteenth century most of Europe was divided between people of the Roman Catholic and Protestant faiths. Believers in one faith found it almost impossible to tolerate members of the other.

Divided Faiths

Here are some of the differences between Roman Catholics and Protestants at the time of Queen Elizabeth:

ROMAN CATHOLICS accepted the Pope as the head of the church. PROTESTANTS called the Pope the 'Bishop of Rome' and would not accept his leadership. Unlike the Church of England, many Protestant churches had no bishops at all.

ROMAN CATHOLICS believed that only through the help of a priest, who was not permitted to marry, could a person go to heaven. PROTESTANTS believed that every individual made his or her own relationship with God. Priests were permitted to marry.

ROMAN CATHOLIC services and Bible were in Latin. PROTESTANTS used their own languages (the vernacular).

ROMAN CATHOLICS believed that statues and paintings could help a person's faith. PROTESTANTS said that such things got in the way of one's relationship with God. They whitewashed over the paintings on the inside of the churches, broke statues of saints and smashed stained glass windows.

The ROMAN CATHOLIC church encouraged men and women to devote their lives to God by entering a monastery or nunnery. PROTESTANTS abolished these institutions. You can still see their ruins in many parts of England and Wales.

ROMAN CATHOLICS believed that, in a special way, Christ was actually present at the service based on His Last Supper, known as the Mass. Some PROTESTANTS saw their communion services as just memorials to the Last Supper. Some of them thought that, since God knows everything, He knows as soon as someone is born whether or not he or she is going to heaven.

CAN YOU REMEMBER ?

What were the main differences between Roman Catholicism and Protestantism?

What was the faith of the following monarchs: Edward VI, Mary I, Elizabeth I?

Who was Elizabeth's first puritan Archbishop of Canterbury?

What was Foxe's Book of Martyrs about?

Why was the Church of England vitally important to Queen Elizabeth?

CHECK YOUR UNDERSTANDING

Can you remember the meaning of the following words?

Heretic	Vernacular
Convert	Martyr
Puritan	Propaganda

THINGS TO DO

1 Look up the word 'Reformation' (with a capital 'R'). What does it mean? How does it apply to Elizabethan England?

2 Next time you are near an old church or cathedral, look carefully to see if you can find damage done when England changed from a Roman Catholic to a Protestant country. What damage might you expect to find?

Propaganda

The differences between the Roman Catholic and Protestant faiths might not seem very important to us, but they were enough to make Elizabethans hate each other. This horrific and exaggerated picture was drawn in 1592 to show how cruel English Protestants were to Roman Catholic priests whom they captured.

What do we mean when we describe such work as propaganda?

More Propaganda

Here is some Protestant propaganda. It is from John Foxe's *Book of Martyrs*, one of the most popular books in Elizabethan England. The work tells how the Roman Catholics killed many Protestants before Elizabeth came to the throne. Foxe describes the burning of Rawlins White:

> Then some that stood by cried out, 'Put fire, set to fire!' which being done, the straw and reeds cast up both a great and sudden flame, in which this good and blessed man kept his hands till the sinews shrunk, and the fat dropped away . . . All this while . . . he cried with a loud voice, 'O Lord receive my soul; O Lord receive my spirit!' until he could not open his mouth. At last the fire burned so vehemently [strongly] against his legs that they were consumed [destroyed] almost before the rest of his body was burned, which made the whole body fall over . . . into the fire sooner than it would have done. Thus died this godly old man Rawlins . . .

Nowadays, through elections to parliament and local councils, all adults have a say in how they are governed. We call this democracy. Most Elizabethans had no such choice. The country was a monarchy; that is to say, the queen governed in the way she thought best, like a headmaster or headmistress of a school. She was expected to listen to the advice of her important and powerful subjects, but in the end everyone had to do what she said.

However, most Elizabethans never saw the queen and they knew little of what she and her ministers decided. Their day to day lives were controlled by local authorities. These were the village constables, churchwardens and, most important of all, the Justices of the Peace (JPs or magistrates). These men were responsible for a host of tasks, from seeing that roads and bridges were maintained to ensuring that everyone went to church. They held their own law courts where offenders were tried and punished. The church also had local courts, responsible for dealing with moral offences, such as swearing. The whole country was also divided into diocese, each one supervised by a bishop, who had his own court. A Lord Lieutenant looked after his county. County courts dealt with more important crimes. The queen and her ministers kept in touch with JPs, Lords Lieutenant and bishops through an endless stream of letters, orders and messages.

Elizabeth governed with the help of a small group of ministers known as the Privy Council. The most important ministers were the Lord Chancellor, the Lord Treasurer and the Secretary of State. Throughout almost her entire reign Elizabeth was served by William Cecil. He was her principal minister, acting as Secretary from 1558 to 1572 and Treasurer from 1572 until his death in 1598.

The Privy Council met almost every day, advising the queen on the decisions she had to take and dealing with unimportant matters for which she did not have time. As a guarantee that they were genuine, all the queen's orders and written decisions were stamped in wax with the royal seal.

Elizabeth also summoned a parliament when she needed to. This was an ancient institution made up of two parts or 'houses'. The nobles were entitled to sit in the 'upper house', the House of Lords. The 'lower house', or House of Commons, was made up of two representatives from every county and important town. These towns were known as boroughs and had certain privileges given to them in a royal charter.

Parliament had three functions. It had the right to grant extra taxation when the government needed more money, for example in wartime. Secondly, its approval was required for important new laws, called statutes. The Church of England was founded in 1559 by two parliamentary statutes. Finally, parliament was a useful meeting point between the queen's government and representatives of her people. She could let them know what she wanted. In turn, they could tactfully inform her if they had any complaints (known as grievances). Most of the time this partnership worked quite well.

Two peers (lords) and a soldier. In Elizabethan times the small number of wealthy and privileged nobles played a major part in the government of the realm.

Een Grave ot Lord
van den Parlemente

Een Lord van
der ordre, zoo hy
ghecleedt
gaet op St
Joeris dach

Eenen ridder
onder der
Majesteit

A Procession

Queen Elizabeth loved ceremony. This is a foreigner's description of her procession to open parliament in 1584. Why do you think it was necessary for her to appear magnificent at times like this?

All the streets and lanes in Westminster were well cleaned and strewn with sand when the queen made her entrance . . . At the head of the procession rode, two by two, eighteen lords and gentlemen of the court, after them fifteen trumpets [trumpeters], two gentlemen, each with 100 soldiers uniformly clad; now came fifteen members of parliament in long red cloth coats, lined with white rabbit . . . [after many more figures] Now followed the queen in a half-covered sedan chair*, which looked like a half-covered Bed. The chair and cushions on which the queen was seated were covered with gold and silver cloth. The queen had a long red velvet parliamentary mantle, down to the waist, lined with ermine, white with little black dots, and a crown on her head. The sedan chair was carried by two cream-coloured horses . . .

*sedan chair = a chair on poles which can be carried about.

Bearing in mind how most people lived in Elizabethan times, you can imagine how striking the spectacle was.

Taxation

Despite making such a fine impression, Elizabeth did not always get her own way in parliament. In 1593 the country was at war with Spain and English soldiers were fighting in France. The queen asked for extra taxation to help pay for war. Sir Francis Bacon had his doubts:

For impossibility: the poor men's rent is such that they are not able to yield [pay] it . . . The gentlemen must sell their plate [tableware], the farmers their brass pots, ere [before] this will be paid . . . The dangers are these. We shall first breed discontentment in paying these subsidies [taxes], and . . . endanger her Majesty's safety, which must consist more in the love of the people than in their wealth . . .

(From Sir Simmonds O'Ewes, *Journal of all the Parliaments During the Reign of Queen Elizabeth*)

CHECK YOUR UNDERSTANDING

Can you remember the meaning of the following words?

Monarchy

Justice of the Peace

Diocese

Lord Lieutenant

Royal seal

Borough

Pillory

Subsidy

Q

What was Bacon saying might happen if the government went ahead and collected the taxes?

What do you think was Elizabeth's reaction to such a speech?

Do you think it helped the government if MPs were able to speak their minds like this?

Crime and Punishment

A pillory (left) and stocks, two common instruments of punishment in Elizabethan times. For minor offences men and women were sentenced to public humiliation by being locked into these devices. Can you see how they worked?

Petty criminals were dealt with by the JP. But a local justice was not always honest, as one MP pointed out in 1601:

A Justice of Peace is a Living Creature*, that [who] for half a dozen of chickens will Dispense [ignore] with a whole Dozen of Penal Statutes*.

Living Creature = someone who is keen to make a good living; *Penal Statutes* = laws regarding criminals.

(From H. Townshend, *Historical Collections*)

Justice in Elizabethan England was not always carried out in a fair and unbiased manner.

What corruption is the JP being accused of here?

THINGS TO DO

1 Draw a simple diagram showing the key figures in Elizabethan government. Include the following: queen, privy council, lords lieutenant, bishops, justices of the peace, constables.

2 Find out how often Elizabeth summoned a parliament during her reign.

3 Make a list of the punishments used for law breakers in Elizabethan times.

4 In which of Shakespeare's plays do we find Justice Shallow? What do you think Shakespeare was hinting at by giving him that name?

CAN YOU REMEMBER ?

Which small group of ministers helped the queen govern the country?

What types of local court were there in Elizabethan England?

What were the functions of parliament?

Did MPs always agree with Elizabeth?

How do we know that justice was not always fairly administered?

In the eyes of many Roman Catholics Elizabeth I was not the true queen of England. They believed that when Elizabeth was born, Henry VIII was still married to his first wife, Catherine of Aragon, so Elizabeth was illegitimate and unable to succeed to the throne. In fact Henry had established his own church and persuaded the Archbishop of Canterbury to grant him a divorce from Catherine. As the Roman Catholics could not accept this, they considered Elizabeth's cousin, Mary Queen of Scots, to be the true Queen of England.

Mary was a Roman Catholic but an incompetent ruler. In 1568 she was driven out of her northern kingdom by the Scots and sought refuge in England. Elizabeth did not know what to do. She felt obliged to show some courtesy to her royal cousin, but it soon became clear that Mary was scheming to replace Elizabeth on the English throne. The Elizabethan age was thick with codes, spies and plots, many of them centring around Mary. She kept in touch with Roman Catholic noblemen in England, as well as the Pope and the kings of Roman Catholic France and Spain.

The most serious plot in which Mary was involved took place in 1569. The Earls of Northumberland and Westmorland gathered their followers and rose in rebellion. They said that they wanted to restore the Roman Catholic religion. Their rebellion was a test of Elizabeth's government. The earls were old-fashioned barons, almost mini-kings, with their own castles and retainers. There was no place for such people in Elizabethan England, where power lay with the queen and her privy council of ministers. The revolt of the northern earls failed. Hundreds were executed as a warning from Elizabeth of what happened to those who challenged her authority. Eventually, eighteen years later, Mary Queen of Scots was executed too.

Elizabeth had no regular troops with which to put down the northern rebellion. She was always hard-up and could not afford to keep soldiers in case they might be needed. She raised an army only when it was required, and when she did so it put a huge strain on her finances. She had to ask parliament for extra taxes. This could lead to problems, as we have seen (page 38).

Elizabeth fought two small wars early in her reign, one in Scotland and the other in France. She then decided to avoid war if she possibly could. Eventually, however, in 1585 she was forced to help the Dutch in their struggle with Spain. This led to a long, expensive and not always successful war, which later spilled over into fighting in France and Ireland. There were one or two moments of triumph, as when in 1588 the queen's navy defeated the Spanish Armada. But for much of the time the war meant high taxation at a time when things were already hard – there were poor harvests 1594–1597. And for the unfortunate men who served in the navy or army the war brought danger, hardship and, all too often, death.

English forces attacking the Spanish port of Cadiz in 1587. Large-scale raids of this type were | *very expensive and difficult to organize. Notice the large Spanish ships powered by oars (galleys).* | *Why do you think that the English did not favour this design of ship?*

PLOT, REBELLION AND WAR

The Throckmorton Plot

In 1583 the agents of Elizabeth's Secretary, Sir Francis Walsingham, uncovered a dangerous plot by Francis Throckmorton. In this extract the traitor explains that the French Roman Catholic nobleman, the Duke of Guise, was to lead a rebellion, using his own troops. Throckmorton also explains that the secret aim of the rebellion was to overthrow Elizabeth:

> . . . The Duke of Guise should be the principal leader and executor* of that invasion. That the pretension which should be publicly notified* should be to deliver the Scottish Queen to liberty, and to procure [get], even by force, from the Queen [Elizabeth] . . . a tolerance in religion for . . . Catholics; but the intention . . . [which] should not at first be made known to all men, should be, upon the Queen's . . . resistance, to remove her . . . from her crown . . .
>
> *executor = the person who is going to carry it out; *the pretension which should be publicly notified* = the aim which people will be told of.

Whom do you imagine the conspirators wished to put on the English throne in place of Elizabeth? Armed with evidence such as this, Elizabeth was forced to execute Mary in 1587. This made the hostility of Roman Catholic France and Spain even more bitter.

The Cost of War

The English queen's reluctance to go to war is made clear in these figures for the year 1600. It was estimated that the government's income would be £374,000. Now consider what her military expenses would be:

	£
Treasurer to the Navy	2000
Victualling [supplying] the navy	15,000
Lieutenant of the Ordnance [responsible for weapons]	6000
Master of the armoury	400
Lieutenant of the Tower	2000
Castles etc	4000
Ireland [where English troops were fighting]	320,000
Low Countries [Belgium and Holland] [where English troops were fighting]	25,000
TOTAL	374,400

(From *Calendar of State Papers Domestic, Elizabeth*)

In other words, the queen had to spend all her income on military matters, leaving nothing for the ordinary expenses of government. When these were taken into account she had a deficit (the amount owing) of £85,440.

CAN YOU REMEMBER ?

Who was the first wife of Henry VIII?

When did Mary Queen of Scots arrive in England?

Who rebelled against Elizabeth in 1569?

What were the real and pretended aims of the Throckmorton plot?

How much of Elizabeth's income was spent on military matters in 1600?

CHECK YOUR UNDERSTANDING

Can you remember the meaning of the following words?

Galley	Epidemic
Victualling	Musket
Ordnance	Deficit

42

Life in the Forces

The life of an ordinary soldier was terribly hard. Men were poorly paid and their wages were often months late. They could be flogged or even executed without trial for minor offences. Weapons inflicted horrible wounds and English armies were not backed by competent medical services. Study the weapons in the picture below and imagine the sort of injuries they could produce.

Both on board ship and in the army disease was a greater danger than the enemy. It was not uncommon for an army to be unable to fight because so many of its men had been struck down by an epidemic (widespread attack) of typhoid.

Understandably, men were unwilling to join the forces. They had to be bribed or forced into the army or navy. When war broke out recruiting officers went round the jails and houses of correction to find soldiers. As a result, an Elizabethan army was made up of the dregs of society.

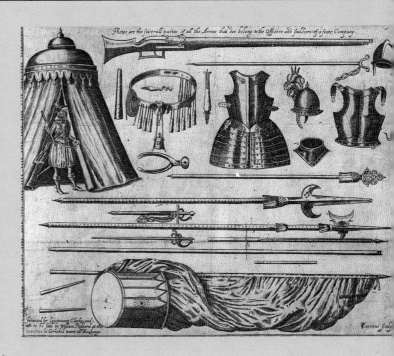

A naval battle. Although cannon could inflict severe damage on a vessel and injure many of the crew, *it was almost impossible to sink a wooden ship with gunfire.*

THINGS TO DO

1   Using the pictures in this section, draw as many different types of Elizabethan soldier as you can, labelling them and explaining each man's task in the army.

2   Find out all you can about the Spanish Armada and, using a map, tell the story of its defeat. What would you say was the main reason why it failed?

3   Write a letter home from an English foot soldier serving in Ireland in 1600.

TIME CHART

1533	Elizabeth born.
1534	Henry VIII (Elizabeth's father) establishes the Church of England.
1549	England's first Protestant Prayer Book introduced.
1553–58	Reign of Elizabeth's Roman Catholic sister, Mary I.
1558	Elizabeth becomes queen.
1559	A Protestant Church of England established.
1560	English forces sent to Scotland.
1562	Elizabeth very ill with smallpox.
	English forces fighting in France.
1563	Foxe's *Book of Martyrs* published.
1566	Longleat House, a fine Elizabethan mansion, begun in Somerset.
1568	Mary Queen of Scots flees to England.
1569	Rebellion of the northern earls.
1571	Harrow School founded.
1572	A system of rates introduced to support the poor.
1574	Roman Catholic priests arrive in England.
1577	Archbishop Grindal suspended from his position.
1577–80	Francis Drake sails round the world.
1585	English troops sent to fight Spain in the Netherlands.
1586	Babington plot to murder Elizabeth.
1587	Mary Queen of Scots executed.
	Puritans try to set up their own church.
1588	Spanish Armada defeated.
1589	English troops sent to France to help the Protestant King Henry IV.
1593	Serious rebellion in Ireland.
1594–97	Bad harvests cause widespread misery.
1597	Shakespeare writes *Romeo and Juliet*.
1599	Globe Theatre built in London.
1601	Poor Laws reorganized.
1603	Queen Elizabeth dies.

ENGLAND AND WALES ABOUT 1600

■ Towns with a population of more than 5000 by 1603
● Other important towns

Main navigable rivers

Main roads

SCOTLAND

Glasgow
Edinburgh
Berwick

Newcastle
Carlisle
Durham

Keswick
Kendal
Kirkby Lonsdale
Ripon
York

Isle of Man

Leeds
Hull
Wakefield

IRELAND

Liverpool
Manchester
Lincoln

Anglesey

Chester
Buxton
Nottingham
Lynn
Yarmouth

IRISH SEA

Oswestry
Stafford
Norwich
Shrewsbury
Lichfield
Thetford
Leicester
Burleigh
House
Dunwich
Coventry
Northampton
Cambridge

WALES
Worcester
Stratford
Ipswich

Cardigan
Banbury
Colchester
Carmarthen
Brecon
Burford
St Albans
Gloucester
Oxford
Chelmsford
Abingdon
Cardiff
Malmsbury
Windsor
London
Bristol
Newbury
Maidstone
Canterbury
Bath
Nonsuch
Palace
Dover
Longleat House
Salisbury
Rye
Barnstaple
Portsmouth
Southampton
Chichester
Exeter
Isle of Wight
Totnes
Plymouth
ENGLISH CHANNEL

45

GLOSSARY

Archery   Shooting with bows and arrows

Architecture   The design of buildings

Capital city   A country's chief city

Baron   An important lord

The Continent   The British expression for mainland Europe

Corporal punishment   Physical punishment, such as beating

Courtesy   Kindly and well-mannered behaviour

Devout   Deeply religious

Employee   Someone who is employed by another person

Formal   According to certain rules, traditional

Garrison   A military post

Gentry   The class of people below the nobility; gentlemen

Hamlet   A small village

Jousting   Fighting, usually on horseback, for sport

Latin   The language of the ancient Romans

Literature   Anything written that is of good quality

Livestock   Farm animals

Malnutrition   Having a poor or incorrect diet

Mission   A task

Mutilate   To cripple or spoil

Nobility   The upper classes of society who have inherited their wealth and status

Parish   The district looked after by a priest

Pauper   A very poor person

Philosophy   The study of the real meaning of things

Profession   A job which requires careful academic training, such as a doctor

Pope   The head of the Roman Catholic church

The Reformation   The sixteenth-century movement in which the Christian church split between Protestants and Roman Catholics

Remedy   A cure

Retainer   A servant

Rural   Connected with the countryside

Sentence   Punishment given by a law court

Spinning   Twisting wool into thread

Scurvy   A disease caused by a lack of important vitamins

Tax(ation)   Money paid to the government for running the country

Traitor   Someone who betrays their country

What Can You Remember?

How many people lived in England and Wales during the reign of Elizabeth I?

Was the size of the population rising or falling?

What is the name of the document, granted by the monarch, which gave a town the right to send two representatives to parliament?

How were most houses built in Elizabethan times?

What is the name of the mansion which William Cecil built for himself?

Who controlled an Elizabethan household?

Which ancient language were children at some grammar schools expected to speak all the time?

What was the punishment for being an able-bodied rogue?

For which type of painting were Elizabethan artists famous?

Name three plays by William Shakespeare.

List three differences between the Protestant and Roman Catholic faiths in Elizabethan times.

Who was Elizabeth's chief minister?

Which organization had to approve new taxes?

Why did Elizabeth try to avoid war for so long?

What sort of person ended up in the queen's armed forces?

FURTHER READING

Acland, Robin, Birt, David and Nichol, Joh, *The Tudors*, Edward Arnold.

Cox, Angela, *Sir Henry Unton, Elizabethan Gentleman*, Cambridge.

Jones, Madeline, *Finding Out About Tudor and Stuart Towns*, Batsford.

McDowell, David, *The Spanish Armada*, Batsford.

Palmer, Michael, *Elizabeth I*, Batsford.

Regan, Geoffrey, *Living Through History: Elizabethan England*, Batsford.

Speed, Peter and Mary, *The Elizabethan Age* (four books), Longman.

Steele, Anne and Barry, *How They Lived: A Tudor Merchant*, Wayland.

Watson, Roger, *At the Time of Mary, Queen of Scots*, Longman.

White-Thomson, Stephen, *Elizabeth I and Tudor England*, Wayland.

Acknowledgements

The Author and Publishers would like to thank the following for permission to reproduce illustrations: Archivo Fotografico for pages 40–41; The Bridgeman Art Library for pages 5, 13, 16–17, 23, 25, 32–33 and 37; The Fitzwilliam Museum, Cambridge for pages 28–29; The Mansell Collection for page 30; J. S. Ross for pages 10, 20–21 and 39, The Royal Collection for the frontispiece. Other illustrations supplied by the Publisher. The map was drawn by Mr M. Chabou.

INDEX

Numbers in **bold type** refer to
illustrations